Killer Plants
and how to grow them

Gordon Cheers & Julie Silk

Illustrated by
Marjorie Crosby-Fairall

Puffin Books

For Daniel and Hannah,
with love, GC and JS

For Geoff and my folks,
love, MACF

Puffin Books
Penguin Books Australia Ltd
487 Maroondah Highway, PO Box 257
Ringwood, Victoria 3134, Australia
Penguin Books Ltd
Harmondsworth, Middlesex, England
Viking Penguin, A Division of Penguin Books USA Inc.
375 Hudson Street, New York, New York 10014, USA
Penguin Books Canada Limited
10 Alcorn Avenue, Toronto, Ontario, Canada M4V 3B2
Penguin Books (N.Z.) Ltd
182–190 Wairau Road, Auckland 10, New Zealand

First published by Penguin Books Australia, 1996

1 3 5 7 9 10 8 6 4 2

Text Copyright © Gordon Cheers and Julie Silk, 1996
Illustrations Copyright © Marjory Crosby-Fairall, 1996

All rights reserved. Without limiting the rights under copyright reserved above, no part of this publication may be reproduced, stored in or introduced into a retrieval system, or transmitted, in any form or by any means (electronic, mechanical, photocopying, recording or otherwise), without the prior written permission of both the copyright owner and the above publisher of this book.

Typeset in 16/20 Bembo
Made and printed in Australia by Southbank Book

National Library of Australia
Cataloguing-in-Publication data:

Cheers, Gordon, 1954–.
Killer Plants and How to Grow Them

ISBN 0 14 054801 7

1. Carnivorous plants – juvenile literature. 1. Silk, Julie, 1965– . I. Title.

583.121

Words printed in **bold** have more information in the glossary or on other pages.

Christopher Britton.

Contents

Plants that eat meat!   4
How carnivorous plants trap their prey   6
Venus Fly Traps   10
Sundews   12
Albany Pitcher Plants   14
Tall Pitcher Plants   16
Cobra Lilies   18
Monkey Cups   20
Butterworts   22
Bladderworts   23
How big are they?   24
Where in the world?   26
Growing carnivorous plants at home   28
Botanical names   30
Glossary   31
Finding out more   32
Index   32

Plants that eat meat!

People eat plants. Animals eat plants. Insects eat plants. But there are some plants that are not happy just to be someone else's meal – these plants bite back! And unsuspecting creatures wandering too close could find themselves being eaten – by a plant!

These clever plants are called 'carnivorous', which means they eat flesh.

There are many different types of carnivorous plants, and they grow all over the world. Some are so tiny you could easily step on them and never know. Others grow high above the forest floor. Some have traps as big as footballs, and others trap their **prey** with tiny thread-like leaves. They look like ordinary plants – until you see them grab an insect. And that is *not* what ordinary plants do! In fact, it is so strange that when these plants were first discovered, most people didn't believe it. Scientists who said plants could eat insects were laughed at. Imagine everyone's amazement when plants that could eat rats and birds were found!

Strange as they are, though, most of these plants are easy to grow. In this book you will find out about some of the most famous carnivorous plants – how they trap their prey, how big they grow, where they can be found, and even how to grow your own killer plants!

Why do they eat meat?

Most plants are happy to take the **nutrients** they need from the soil. So why are carnivorous plants different? The reason is that most carnivorous plants live in poor soils which are low in some nutrients. Catching animals is their way of finding those missing nutrients. They don't need to eat meat to survive, but it helps them stay healthy in areas where other plants might die.

How carnivorous plants trap their prey

Carnivorous plants attract their victims in the same ways other plants attract insects for **pollination**. Insects are drawn to the bright colours, sweet smells or even the rotten smell of earlier victims. Once the insects have landed, carnivorous plants make sure they cannot escape.

Venus Fly Traps and **Bladderworts** have trigger traps. The Venus Fly Trap has special leaves that spring shut like the jaws of a crocodile. When the trigger hairs are touched twice (within 25 seconds of each other), the trap snaps shut and fills with fluid, drowning the insect.

Venus Fly Trap

Sundews and **Butterworts** have a sticky liquid, like honey, on thin tentacles covering their leaves. An insect landing for a tasty treat soon finds it is stuck. The more it struggles, the more sticky tentacles reach out to trap it. Eventually the whole leaf curls around and engulfs the insect.

Sticky Traps

Sundew

Albany Pitcher Plants and **Monkey Cups** use pitfall traps. Creatures are attracted into the pitchers or cups by the smell or the bright colour. But when they go inside to investigate, they soon find that the sides are too slippery to climb out.

Stuck in the stomach
The prey slide on the slippery sides, eventually falling into the pool of digestive fluid at the bottom where they drown. Then they are dissolved and absorbed by the plant.

Pitfall Traps

Spiky Tunnels

Tall Pitcher Plants and **Cobra Lilies** have spiky tunnels. Flying insects are attracted to the brightly coloured pitchers. After tasting the sweet nectar on the rim, they follow a trail of nectar into the pitcher. The path down is smooth but if the insect tries to go back its escape route is blocked by spiky downward-pointing hairs. The insect goes further and further into the pitcher until finally it falls into the digestive liquid at the bottom.

downward-pointing hairs

Venus Fly Traps

The Venus Fly Trap is named after Venus, the Roman goddess of beauty.

The most famous carnivorous plant is the Venus Fly Trap. It lives in the swamps and bogs of the south-east of North America. These plants grow only to a maximum of 15 cm, but they mean death to any ant, fly or wasp that ventures onto the waiting jaws. The trap reopens after about 10 days, but all that is left of the insect is its hard outer shell, which is soon blown away by the wind. The trap is now ready for another tasty insect.

Too late! The leaves of the Venus Fly Trap can snap shut in less than a second.

Tips for growing

Venus Fly Traps are easy to grow in a sunny spot in damp peat moss. They can be grown from seeds or the plants can be divided at the base and replanted. Each Venus Fly Trap has six traps – if there are twelve traps you actually have two plants. Don't feed your plant dead insects – you might kill it. The plant needs the struggling of the dying insect to release the digestive fluids.

Sundews

Sundews are found in most parts of the world, but more live in Australia than anywhere else. They catch mosquitoes, ants, flies and other small insects. Some Sundews are as small as your fingertip. Others grow up to 60 cm tall. They are called Sundews because the droplets of sticky liquid on the end of the tentacles glisten like dew in the sunlight.

A sticky end
When an insect lands on the plant it becomes glued to the sticky nectar on the tentacles. The more the insect struggles the more tentacles reach out to hold it tight.

Tips for growing

Sundews are the easiest of all carnivorous plants to grow. In a pot on a sunny windowsill they will catch hundreds of flies and crawling insects.

You can grow a new plant from seeds or by removing a leaf from the base of another plant and placing it on damp soil under a glass for 6 weeks.

Sleepy heads
Many Sundews grow in soil that is damp all year round, but some species become **dormant** when the soil dries out in summer.

Albany Pitcher Plants

Albany Pitcher Plants live in a small part of south-western Australia. They have small jug-like pitchers with slippery sides and sharp teeth around the rim. They catch flies, mosquitoes, slugs, ants and slaters.

A 'pitcher' is a special type of container for holding liquids.

Tough guys
The pitchers are small, growing to only about 5 cm high, but they are very strong and can even survive being trampled on by kangaroos who graze around the area in which they grow.

Colour

When grown in full sunlight, the pitchers are dark red. In the shade, they are bright green. Flying insects are more attracted to the red pitchers.

Tips for growing

Albany Pitcher Plants can be grown in damp peat soil. They can be **propagated** from seeds or cuttings. If your plant is not well, it will close its lid. The lid may stay closed until its growing conditions are right again.

Insects are prevented from escaping by the sharp teeth around the rim of the plant's mouth.

Tall Pitcher Plants

Tall Pitcher Plants grow on the east coast of North America. Some are found growing near Venus Fly Traps.

Their brightly coloured pitchers attract bees, wasps and other flying insects. Crawling creatures such as ants and slaters climb up the pitchers, attracted by the sweet-smelling nectar, or by the smell of insects already rotting inside the pitchers.

Greedy!
When the insect tastes nectar on the rim of the pitcher, it crawls down the tunnel looking for more. But once it reaches the bottom, it cannot escape because of the downward-pointing hairs.

Cobra Lilies

The Cobra Lily is found on the west coast of North America and is sometimes called the Californian Pitcher Plant. It is one of the larger carnivorous plants, with pitchers which can grow to 60 cm. Cobra Lilies trap flies, mosquitoes, wasps and crawling creatures such as slaters and ants.

Snakey
With their tall twisted pitchers, puffed-up heads and fangs, they look like a cobra, rearing up ready to strike.

The brightly coloured fangs attract insects.

Tips for growing

Cobra Lilies can be grown in a pot of damp peat moss kept in a shady position. Plant seeds or propagate by dividing at the base. Cobra Lilies like to have their roots kept cool, so water daily with very cold water.

Monkey Cups

Monkey Cups are vines that grow in the tropical forests of South-East Asia. They have jug-shaped pitchers that grow up to 30 cm long and hang from vines that can climb to the top of 15-metre trees. As the pitchers of Monkey Cups grow, they fill with liquid. When the liquid is ready to digest prey, the lid opens and the trap is ready.

Pitchers as pots
In the Philippines and Borneo large Monkey Cup pitchers are sometimes used for cooking rice and vegetables.

A big appetite
Moths, rats and even small birds have been found trapped in the pitchers of Monkey Cups!

Why are they called Monkey Cups?
Because monkeys in the jungle have been seen drinking the liquid from these plants!

Medicine cup
The liquid in an unopened pitcher tastes like mineral water and has been used to cure stomach upsets and eye problems.

Tips for growing

Monkey Cups need warmth and moist air. If you don't live in the tropics, you will need to grow them in a glasshouse. Plant them in damp soil in an empty fish tank. You may need overhead lighting. When they grow too large, cut off the top end of the plant, leaving a few pitchers attached. Plant this into the soil and a new plant will start to grow.

Butterworts

Butterworts live mainly in America but some are common in Europe and Asia. This plant often grows in shady places and traps ants, mosquitoes and flies. The flowers can be purple, blue, yellow or white.

Why is it called a Butterwort?
Because the leaves look as if they have been rubbed with butter. 'Wort' is an old word for 'plant'.

Tips for growing
Butterworts can be grown in a pot sitting in a saucer of water on a windowsill that catches only a few hours' sunlight. If your plant is in the sun all day, it might wilt and die. Sometimes new plants will form on the tips of the leaves. These are called pups. Remove the pups and plant in a pot of their own.

Grease trap!
The butterwort has greasy leaves to trap its prey. When an insect lands on the leaves, the plant covers it with a sickly, sweet-smelling liquid and the insect drowns.

Bladderworts

Although the Bladderwort is one of the smallest carnivorous plants, its amazing trap is the cleverest of all. It is found in most parts of the world, usually growing in ponds or in slow-flowing creeks. Others make their homes in very damp soil. The prey of bladderworts is usually mosquito **larvae** that live in the water around them.

Balloon-like sacs or 'bladders' grow at the roots of the Bladderwort. These bladders are very small – some no bigger than the head of a pin.

Tips for growing

Aquatic Bladderworts can be grown floating in a glass of water on a windowsill or on the surface of a fish tank or pond. Bladderworts that grow in damp soil can be propagated by removing a leaf from the base of the plant and placing it on damp soil under a glass for 8 weeks.

If a small insect swimming past the bladder touches the tiny trigger hairs, the trapdoor swings open. This creates a vacuum inside the bladder, sucking the insect inside. The door snaps shut behind it.

How big are they?

60 cm
50 cm — Cobra Lilies
40 cm
30 cm — Sundews
20 cm
10 cm — Albany Pitcher Plants

Cobra Lilies

Actual size

Carnivorous plants come in many different shapes and sizes, depending on what they are trying to trap. The small plants on the ground usually catch crawling insects. But flying insects are the favourite meal of the taller plants.

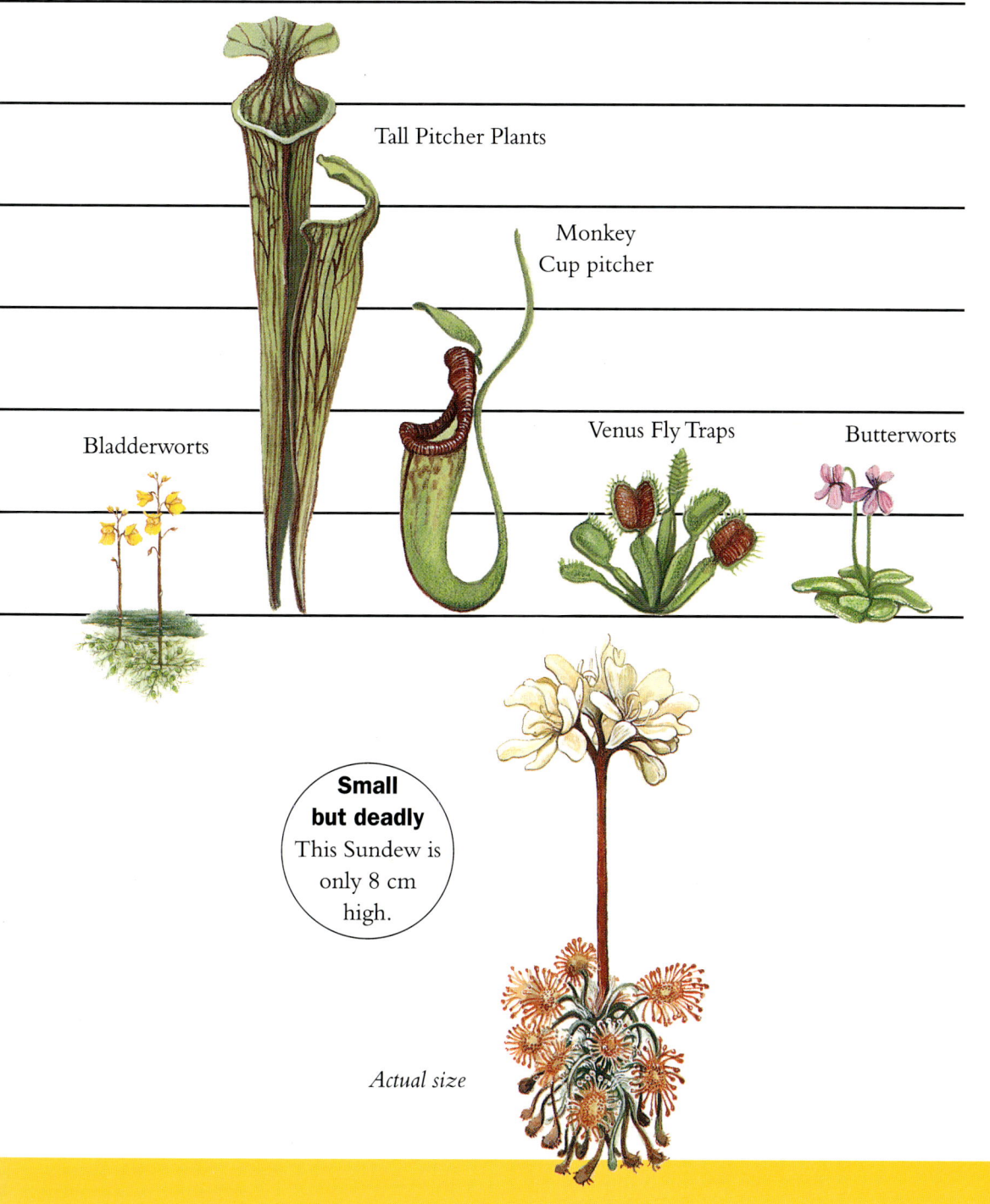

Tall Pitcher Plants

Monkey Cup pitcher

Bladderworts

Venus Fly Traps

Butterworts

Small but deadly
This Sundew is only 8 cm high.

Actual size

Where in the world?

Carnivorous plants are found in almost every part of the world. Some may even be growing in your neighbourhood!

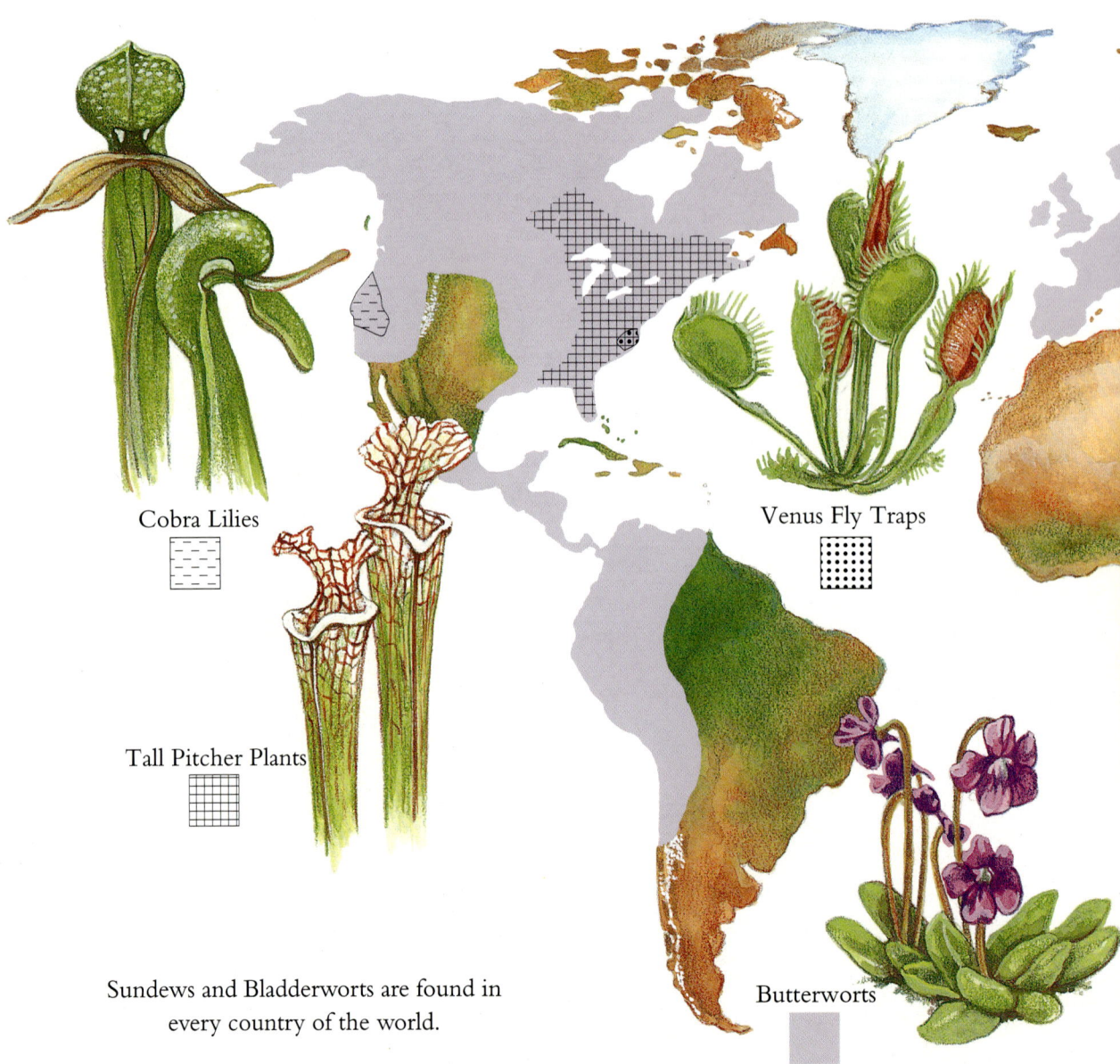

Cobra Lilies

Tall Pitcher Plants

Venus Fly Traps

Butterworts

Sundews and Bladderworts are found in every country of the world.

Growing carnivorous plants at home

Growing carnivorous plants at home is easy. You can buy the right soil and seeds or plants from a nursery. Carnivorous plants can also be propagated by methods such as leaf cuttings and dividing the plant down the middle.

Most of these plants like lots and lots of moisture. Make sure they are in a very sunny position (a sunny windowsill is ideal) and remember to keep the soil very moist. Keeping your pot in a saucer of water is the best way to do this.

Multiplication by division!
Some varieties of carnivorous plants can be propagated by dividing the plant at the bottom near the roots. The Venus Fly Trap will break apart easily into two or more pieces, but for some plants you may need to use a sharp knife or scalpel. Each section of plant can then be repotted. A good soil to use is peat moss, which can be bought at the local nursery.

A miniature greenhouse

To keep their plants warm and moist many people grow these plants in a greenhouse. An unused fish tank with a layer of peat moss makes a good greenhouse if you put a sheet of glass over the top.

Leaf cuttings

To propagate a plant such as a Sundew by leaf cutting, use a scalpel or sharp knife to remove a leaf as close as possible to the bottom of the plant. Lay the leaf in a pot, tentacle side uppermost, flat on the damp soil. A few pins or small pebbles can be used to keep the leaf flat. Next place a glass upside down over the cutting until it sprouts. Using a glass like this is also good when growing plants from seeds.

Botanical names

Most plants have a common name (or nickname) and a botanical (or scientific) name. Just like you have a family name and a first name, botanical names always have a first and second name. But for plants, the first name is a family name and the second is a species name.

There are over 500 different species (types) of carnivorous plants. Below are the botanical names of some of the most popular.

COMMON NAME	BOTANICAL NAME
Venus Fly Trap	*Dionaea muscipula*
Sundew	*Drosera capensis*
	Drosera rotundifolia
	Drosera spathulata
Tall Pitcher Plant	*Sarracenia leucophylla*
	Sarracenia rubra
	Sarracenia purpurea
Monkey Cup	*Nepenthes alata*
	Nepenthes mirabilis
Bladderwort	*Utricularia longifolia*
	Utricularia vulgaris
Butterwort	*Pinguicula caudata*
	Pinguicula moranensis
	Pinguicula vulgaris
Cobra Lily	*Darlingtonia californica*
Albany Pitcher Plant	*Cephalotus follicularis*

Glossary

CARNIVOROUS Meat-eating.

DIGEST To break down food into a form that can be absorbed by the plant or animal.

DORMANT Some plants go into hibernation (just like bears). They don't eat or grow for a period of time such as winter or the dry season. When this happens, the plant is said to be dormant.

LARVAE Insects which have not yet grown into their adult form.

NUTRIENT Any substance needed for plant or animal growth.

POLLINATION When pollen grains from one plant come in contact with others from the same species, causing new seeds to grow. Often this is done by insects flying from flower to flower in search of nectar.

PREY An animal which is caught by another animal or plant for food.

PROPAGATE To grow a new plant from part of another plant.

Finding out more

Here are some books to read to find out more about carnivorous plants:

Gordon Cheers, *Carnivorous Plants* (Carnivor and Insectivor Plants, 1983)
Gordon Cheers, *A Guide to Carnivorous Plants of the World* (Collins Publishers, 1992)
Cynthia Overbeek, *Carnivorous Plants* (Lerner Publications Company, 1982)
John F. Waters, *Carnivorous Plants* (Franklin Watts, 1974)

Index

Albany Pitcher Plants   8, 14–15, 24, 27, 30
Bladderworts   23, 25, 26, 30
Botanical Names   30
Butterworts   22, 25, 26, 30
Cobra Lilies   9, 18–19, 24, 26, 30
Monkey Cups   8, 20–21, 25, 27, 30
Pitfall Traps   8
Spiky Tunnels   9
Sticky Traps   7
Sundews   7, 12–13, 24, 25, 26, 29, 30
Tall Pitcher Plants   9, 16–17, 25, 26, 30
Trigger Traps   6
Venus Fly Traps   6, 10–11, 25, 26, 28, 30